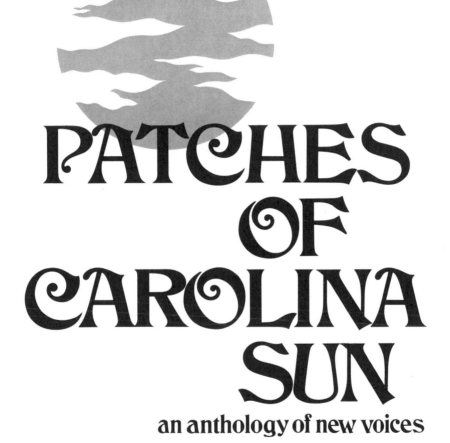

PATCHES OF CAROLINA SUN

an anthology of new voices

PATCHES OF CAROLINA SUN

an anthology of new voices

Edited by

Billy Mishoe, Ph. D.
Ronald G. Midkiff, Ed.D.

American Literary Associates, Inc.
Post Office Box 3321, Columbia, South Carolina 29203

PRODUCTION CREDITS

Dust jacket, production design, and illustration by Beth Moureaux, Talent Associates, Inc., Columbia, South Carolina.

Printed by The State Printing Company, Columbia, South Carolina.

Library of Congress Number 73-85415

Published by

 AMERICAN LITERARY ASSOCIATES, INC.

Post Office Box 3321
Columbia, South Carolina 29203

FOREWORD

There are thousands of amateur writers in South Carolina and the nation who are seeking encouragement and opportunities to share their talents with others. Both the 1972 South Carolina Amateur Poetry Contest and the publication of this volume were in response to these needs. I sincerely hope that those who entered the contest will be encouraged to further develop their creative potential and that those who read *Patches of Carolina Sun* will find it enjoyable.

There are many individuals and organizations who have made invaluable contributions to the success of this effort—friends, school principals and teachers, college professors, newspapers, radio and television stations. Their cooperation and assistance is gratefully acknowledged. I want to thank, especially, the contestants from throughout the state who made this probably the most successful poetry contest in South Carolina history.

Hubert M. Clements, Ed.D.
President
American Literary Associates, Inc.

Columbia, South Carolina
April 9, 1973

Contents

FOREWORD   V

INTRODUCTION   XII

AWARD WINNING POEMS

    For Me   Gerald Gibson   3
    The Death of JoanintheMoon   Philip K. Owen   4
    Ecological Fugue   William Terry Vaughan   5
    Autogenesis   Jan Whalen   6
    Sonnet XII   R. Gordon Bell   7
    Nha Trang   Robert O'Bryan Moffat   8
    Morning Drive   Robert O'Bryan Moffat   9
    To Meinrad   John Hooe   10
    Pregnant   Jill A. King   11
    Untitled   Jill A. King   12
    Minor Meditation on the Insignificance
      of Andrew Wyeth   Lucas Carpenter   13
    Vigil   Idella Bodie   14

MEMORY

    Childhood Calling   Doris M. Herring   17
    Elegy   Karen Joan Segar   18
    Bien Hoa   Robert O'Bryan Moffat   19
    Untitled   Robert O'Bryan Moffat   20
    Cam Rahn   Robert O'Bryan Moffat   21
    Reluctant Volunteer   Samuel Boykin   22
    Generations   Gerald Gibson   23
    The Talisman   Elaine H. Leone   24
    Growing Up So Fast   Lucy G. Laffoday   25
    On Becoming A Man   Philip K. Owen   26
    Sun Tracks   Barbara N. Collins   27
    Last Farewell   Elizabeth Angell Tyson   28

LOVE

Untitled	James E. Burns, Jr.	31
Suppose	Jerry A. Mobley	32
Untitled	Martha Hearon	33
Untitled	Martha Hearon	34
To You	Jan Whalen	35
Untitled	Judy Thompson	36
Growth	William Terry Vaughan	37
Ephemera	Lynn N. Roberson	38
Untitled	Jill A. King	39

ASPIRATION

Four-fingered Glove	William Terry Vaughan	43
Reflection	H. Becton Free	44
Untitled	John Hooe	46
Sonnet XIII	R. Gordon Bell	47
Looking Skyward	Samuel Boykin	48
Lonely Thoughts	H. Becton Free	49
Thoughts on Writing	H. Becton Free	50
Sea Grave	Nell Sharpe	51
A Shrine	Emma R. Bynum	52

OBSERVATIONS

Waiting—A Truckstop Poem	Lance J. Leonhirth	55
Southern Snowfall	Jared C. (Jay) Evatt	56
First Frost	J. R. Long	57
Snow	J. R. Long	58
Untitled	Rhett S. Thurman	59
Shells	Rhett S. Thurman	60
Shooting Rats	Lucas Carpenter	61
Pipe Dream	Lucy G. Laffoday	62
6 O'clock	John Hooe	63
In Salem's Cemetery	R. Gordon Bell	64
The Late Show	Jim R. Bazemore	65

WONDER

Water Unto Water	Gerald W. Smith	69
The Shedding of Skin	Donald R. Belt, Jr.	70
Aquarius	Lucas Carpenter	71
Untitled	Eric Hartley	72
Afternoon With Rain	Lucas Carpenter	73
Imprisoned	Dave Wilson	74
Sunglasses on a Cloudy Day	Dave Wilson	75
Beach—In Winter	Morris C. Lumpkin	76
Idyll For Doe Hall	Kay C. Sisson	77
I Must Have a Place	Grace Pow Simpson	78
This Vital Sea	Grace Pow Simpson	79
Ariadne Abandoned	Terry L. Norton	80
Snowflake	Deck Guess	81

PORTRAITS

A Picture of Parents Without Children	Duane Vorhees	85
The Circle	Rhett S. Thurman	86
His Trowel	Lynn N. Robertson	87
The Fork-Lift	Donald R. Belt, Jr.	88

HUMOR

Untitled	Mabel H. Fischer	91
Great Thinkers, Unite!	Deborah Sue Keister	92
Riddle	Oksanna Nahnybida	93
Girls and Boys	Gerald W. Smith	94
Posthumorous Poem	Gerald W. Smith	95
Umphlettisms	Jerry A. Mobley	96
My Heart Leaps Up When I Behold	Charles G. Joyner	97
Untitled	Charles G. Joyner	98

YOUTH

For I Love Thee	Lori Anne Pierce	101
Beginning: 6:33	Melanie Leigh Boleman	102
The Rosemary	Patricia Wilson	103
Fall	Myrna Gordon	104
Between Snowflakes	Myrna Gordon	105
Icicle Trees	Ellen Deas Boykin	106
Christmas Poem	Brad Kevin Boxey	107
Yesterday	William W. Powell	108
Bumblebees	Ellen Deas Boykin	109
Untitled	Bonnie Campbell	110
My Child	Bonnie Campbell	111
Untitled	Bonnie Campbell	112
Measure Me, Sky	Jerry Charles Bishop	113
Yellow Wednesday's Heroes	Ellen Deas Boykin	114
Swan Sonnet	Ellen Deas Boykin	115
Apple Core	Ellen Deas Boykin	116
Alone	Martha Montgomery Rhodes	117
Childhood	Robin Barnett	118
Daydreams	Julia White	119
Meditation on Myself	Susie Strickland	120
Untitled	Brad Byce	121
Epitaph	Bonnie Campbell	122
Untitled	Tim Hedgecoth	123
Recycling Day	Genie Floyd	124
Simon	Ellen Deas Boykin	125
Indian Charlie and His Arrow	Ellen Deas Boykin	126
A Tribute to Albert Einstein	Deborah Sue Keister	127
Poseidon	Kemp Dudley Box	128

INTRODUCTION

If this volume has any unity, it is the unity of diversity, for the "new voices" are those of businessmen, housewives, college professors, students, and children and their subjects are as varied as their backgrounds. Some of the poems are celebrations and some are lamentations; some express a yearning for the future and some a desire to recapture the past; some focus on love and its promises and some on death and its mysteries. *Patches of Carolina Sun* is evidence that today, as in all ages, men turn to poetry to record their deepest thoughts, their most puzzling questions, their greatest outbursts of joy, their most solemn prayers, and their tenderest feelings.

American Literary Associates, Inc. is responsible for bringing together such variety, for the volume is an epilogue to the 1972 South Carolina Amateur Poetry Contest. From approximately eight hundred entries, those included here were judged the best, not because they represent the kind of poetry most admired by the judges, but because they "most effectively accomplished what they set out to do." Thus, there are poems in the most traditional of forms; there are those that experiment with form and diction; and there are those that, in their childhood simplicity, show promise of further success.

The editing has certainly been an enjoyable experience, for the same reasons that reading the collection should prove enjoyable. We have been reminded that poetry is as real and personal as it has ever been. We have found among South Carolinians concerns and questions that are as timeless as the pleas of Job or the hymns of David, and we have found other concerns as timely as the latest news bulletin. And, finally, we have enjoyed the flavor of South Carolina that permeates the subjects, the images, and the scenes as well as the vocabulary and diction of the poetry. We are sure, for example, that many readers will relive moments of their past, as we have, when they read poems like "For You" and that many will recall the "long, long thoughts" of youth as they read the works submitted by young people from eight to eighteen.

We have also approached the job of editing with a great deal of care. We feel that such things as punctuation, capitalization, rhyme, and phraseology are concerns of the individual poet; and we have revised only when we have been sure that misspellings, omissions, and insertions were not intended.

In organizing the volume we have tried to emphasize the variety that makes it such a patchwork of Carolina experience and thought. Those poems that won first, second, and third place honors and the seven poets who received honorable mention are grouped together with no thematic divisions; the others have been grouped to show man remembering, man wondering, man aspiring, man loving, man learning through observation, man commenting on his fellow man, and man laughing at himself and life. The final section includes poems written by secondary and elementary school students. Within the grouping, there are no thematic sub-divisions, but there is a great deal of variety. Indeed, we think the reader will be reminded, as we have, of Longfellow's translation from the *Kalevala:* "The thoughts of youth are long, long thoughts."

B. M., R. G. M.

Award Winning Poems

"suspiring spires of pines
poke heavenward, and over them
hawks swim the wind."

FOR ME

Look where beagles leap up friendly
from their porch-sleep, where
pork-rich pintos bubble savory
on backs of stoves, where
fireplace stockings pend in wide-mouthed expectation, where
lamps light red crayolas waxing valentines for
girls too elegant to love.
Look where tongues hunt pesky popcorn husks
in picture-show dark, where
noses press cold candy-counter glass, where
fingers grub impatient in black mud for fat pink worms, where
ears catch mouth-harp lamentation celebrating Saturday, where
eyes track fast green apples flung through dusk at
too-swift velvet bats.
Look where country stores squat by crossroads,
hiding garrulous broods of red-neck men
under the shade of their wings, where
churches fold prayer-hands
over the heads of soap-cleansed congregations
and hurl high crosses
onto the cumulus froth.
Look where clay hills hump their blushing backs
under the shimmering heat waves
and creeks run crystal
under the quivering portraits of fish-bone ferns, where
suspiring spires of pines
poke heavenward, and over them
hawks swim the wind.

GERALD GIBSON
Charleston, S. C.
FIRST PLACE WINNER

The Death of Joaninthemoon

If I'd taken one more   step   to the right
    before I released the shot between the forks
        of the twig
            of the branch
                of the limb
(I can still see the fringed fragrance of the
    pinkblackblossoms)   on the mimosa
Fringed flagella   pulled   the shot   (malignant mimosa)
    otherwise I'd have hit the   Maninthemoon right
    between the eyes with my stone but I didn't
        take the step and there were
        the flagella   theflagella   the flagella
And the Maninthemoon suddenly   fell
    from the black
        on his back
            in the road
(and she was Joaninthemoon) with a hole right between
    the eyes from my stone and a   Voice   behind me was
    screaming What have you   done   What have you   done
I took one   step   to the right
    and pointed to the mimosa flagella but they had
        disappeared in the black and the   Voice   was
        only staring at Joaninthemoon
    on her back
        in the black
            on the road
with a hole right between the eyes from my stone
        anyway

PHILIP K. OWEN
Bob Jones University
Greenville, S. C.
SECOND PLACE WINNER

Ecological Fugue

We wither within rivers and fens become bloated
with beerbottles bled of deadly brew while eyes despise
sulphurous skies incest of waste and whory-looking landscape
ears hear yet fear clatter of cans amid clash of trash
matter that fans phantasmagoria of filth formed from
    refuse misuse and non-use in hideous cities
confuses issues from chugging chimneys clogged with smog—
Sing a song of profit and gain, margin and cost,
                brother Faust.

Blood red moons rise and swoon in sulphurous skies
where haste makes waste and flies feed over phantasmagoric fens
noise enjoys beerbottle landscape
    and rape of river incested by crash of cans
wearies the ears
trash dashes from hideous hands piteous pans
    and villainous vans
excuse refuse which when in chimneys charred
dries our eyes and abuses tissues
coated and drugged from smoggy brew all groggy—
Sing a song of advance and development, financing the loss,
                brother Faust.

Gutters are cluttered forming montage of garbage
matter is scattered becoming collage of sewage
tissues congested and issues infested cause lungs to be arrested
atmosphere of smoke makes hearts choke with spasms of fear
cacophonic din and sonic boom bring
ulcers and hypertonic pulses amid catatonic wind
tarnished sun bewails his eye all bloodshot
as we wither within rivers of varnish and rot—
Sell our souls to death and destruction, tempest and toss,
                brother Faust.

WILLIAM TERRY VAUGHAN
University of S. C.
Columbia, S. C.
THIRD PLACE WINNER

AUTOGENESIS

It used to be that I could stand on
  a windswept hill
And with eyes unshaded, count each
  golden daffodil!

Now that I am older and wiser
  I need a visor.

JAN WHALEN
Columbia, S. C.
HONORABLE MENTION

Sonnet XII

While Day was in her dressing room, in that
Brief space of time when she undoes her gowns
Of light and drops them to the floor, I sat
In pleats of fallen clothes of varied browns
And greens, and viewed her splendid nakedness,
A beauty unsurpassed. She smoothed just then
Her cloudy slip with one prolonged caress.
Her fingers were a rosy pink, and men
Have never known the touch of them, though all
Must wish they had. She donned her evening dress
Of black, untied her hair and let it fall,
Then fixed a wealth of stars to every tress.
I left unnoticed, turning for a peep
At how in silence, Day fell fast asleep.

R. GORDON BELL
The Citadel
Charleston, S. C.
HONORABLE MENTION

nha trang

before the dawn
    the mountains were blacked out
i sat watching the foreign sunlight
  erase the error

through the shuttered window
i saw palms caress the
        hillside
            soothing the wound
                of night rocks

ROBERT O'BRYAN MOFFAT
Williamston, S. C.
HONORABLE MENTION

morning drive

electric
     marches in dumb cortege
   among the leaves of morning
and along the asphalt ribbon
    paper is split
      stirred
         and reopened

millers and bud
    frolic
    roll
      and tumble
   in plum bush and
     melon patch
       to the tune of
        a chimney flute
          above the johnson grass
       which becomes springtime
       with salem
      alive and young
       with pepsi
     as we live in our
       old new frontier
         and our
       discarded great society
         in garbaged bliss
       awaiting the generation of peace

ROBERT O'BRYAN MOFFAT
Williamston, S. C.
HONORABLE MENTION

to Meinrad

        One
              dry
needle
              after
                  another

clicks its end
among fancy paper gifts;
an offering sapped of joy
as quickly as sugarwater-spikes
draw forth
the last wasteful gushes
of life-blood.

On simple, branched trunk
complimented not even by twelve,
evergreen cones,
remains only the pining,
hand crafted work of embellishment.
A work of love
first faithfully mounted
for all people to see.

And atop,
an angel shines round about.
Her majestic aura,
            chanced on one dry needle upon another,
            slandered by crusty red of
                      aging ornament,
softly filters mantel scenes
of swaddling clothes
and tender corpses of proud young pigeons

penetrating the nightwalls
with good tidings of great joy.

JOHN HOOE
Wofford College
Spartanburg, S. C.
HONORABLE MENTION

Pregnant

I AM

a gas balloon

bulbous breasts

bulging belly

lumbering longing

in drugged dreams

to become again

a

r
e
e
d

a
c
r
a
n
e

!

JILL A. KING
Florence, S. C.
HONORABLE MENTION

I would drink wine
from a rose
or from lips
quite as red
against me
I would press
the flaming sun
the fevered breast
for one night
of mortal love
I would forfeit
a million more
to the arms
of death then
forbid human grief
to place a wreath
at my grave

JILL A. KING
Florence, S. C.
HONORABLE MENTION

MINOR MEDITATION ON THE INSIGNIFICANCE OF ANDREW WYETH

Away from any well-thought, rising city
find a meager, wispy sky
over a junked-out Chrysler,
a Chrysler alone in a corner of a yellow field of hay straw,
a field alone with its man-natural ravaged automobile.
Things with a past, past objects judged.
No revelation.
Then it is about a shredded sky, an automobile,
and judgments made after the red book of beasts,
the grey-dappled dictionary of objects, judgments
obviated by their pointed incompleteness. A German
notes incertitude with certainty, rises from his desk,
and moves to an armchair in his well-settled home
where a potted plant dies silently in a corner.
Any beginning sends its end out . . . .

Mirrors and the eyes of men are the only world reflectors,
and even so the reflection is made in fragments.
To be aware of the other side of the Chrysler,
of what lies beyond the corner of the field,
even beneath that same wispy sky, is to be aware, is to see
only as we know more than is seen.

LUCAS CARPENTER
Charleston, S. C.
HONORABLE MENTION

Vigil

Vulnerable, I sit by your high white bed.
Eons away antiseptic voices move on soleless shoes
    along corridors swabbed glasslike.
Colorless light rays invade our world, slanting across
    your body and framing it frail beneath the sheet.
With each labored surge of breath and cadenced beat of heart
I am unsheathed — peeled raw.
All insulation stripped, I taste the pain of naked love.
My heart is strung out — hewn to a taut line.

IDELLA BODIE
Aiken, S. C.
HONORABLE MENTION

Memory

"O, I am wrapped in time's afghan today"

CHILDHOOD CALLING

O, I am wrapped in time's afghan today
And dream again of childhood, far away
And ache for country's sights and smells
Of honeysuckle bush and sweet williams thrown upon
Straw-covered hills,
With dog-tooth violets sprinkled beneath a sweet shrub bush
I long for my beloved country hills away from city's rush,
The clean taste of country air breathed in,
The tang of wild haw juice upon my chin.

I was not born to live in city dwelling
But made to see the wild trees' springtime buds a-swelling,
And hear the whippoorwill moan as he calls his own name
"Whip-poor-will," an introduction all night 'til the fervent
Child-sleep came.
"Whip-poor-will" in answer to the screech owl's "whoo,"
And look! a mocking bird! no telling what he will do!
Once in country you have seen humming bird's helicopter
Body whir upon a bachelor's button
And watched tight green pods turn brown to burst with cotton,
Seen purple violets peek from beneath honeysuckle's pink skirt,
And pine straw, a patchwork quilt upon the dirt,
White clouds of dogwood float amid the trees,
And wildflower's heady scent bring an orchestra of bumblebees,
You'll know why time can never take from me
My childhood's wildflower scented memory.
O, I am glad I grew up in the wild
And danced the loving hills as a child.

DORIS M. HERRING
Columbia, S. C.

ELEGY

Memories . . .
Their golden elegance
Softly splendored
In childhood's fibers . . .
Everyday living
Antiqued in thoughts
Which mellow
Like the sun's caress,
Gently shrouded
In black pearl.

KAREN JOAN SEGAR
Bob Jones University
Greenville, S. C.

bien hoa

i remember walking into heat
  and seeing brown

dust became pierced with green swords
      the heat rippled like water
                struck with clay rocks
and smoke splashed the sky

the door closed
and my world flew away
    like a great bird migrating
         in the spring

ROBERT O'BRYAN MOFFAT
Williamston, S. C.

forests
    where war never ends
stand against gray sky smoke
and tracer light

    tranquil combat of nature
               and man
       takes to bullets
         and they are like grasshoppers
           from rock to air
        where steel bird eggs fly
         fall and break

craters from practiced fury
    sink from the swiss cheese
        covering

ROBERT O'BRYAN MOFFAT
Williamston, S. C.

cam rahn

mounds of sugar sour in the sun
   while i walk at night
artificial light pushes me down
      into the ferment
   i catch steel briars
    and bleed for safety
      yet sink into the waterless mire
       trapped for a great white bird
      to prey upon

ROBERT O'BRYAN MOFFAT
Williamston, S. C.

21

RELUCTANT VOLUNTEER

Shrouded by a mist
The firemen's band
Playing patriotic ditties
Ephemeral as the relic
I see trekking through
My mind,
Clad in faded leggings
Left over from a faded War
. . . To End All Wars.

The sad wrinkled doughboy
But heralds onslaught
By endless grey columns
Filled with unsmiling faces
Chanting well-worn slogans of
A safe world for democracy,
A democracy for these dead
Left over from faded Wars
. . . To End All Wars.

Faceless bodies streaming by
Fluid as guidons above them
Beckoning silently to me
From their column of the dead
Revealing that one is absent
And my heart screams
With the knowing
That I am the truant from
Just Another War
. . . To End All Wars.

SAMUEL BOYKIN
Seneca, S. C.

GENERATIONS

I remember it well:
the way the last-light fell
through the wavy window-glass
pushing the gathering shadows aside
to find their faces.
The rocker pair moved, creaking,
just out of phase,
and the old man chewed his
Ripe Peach wad
in perfect time. They spoke,
drawling up familiar names
of unknown men
and never-known times
that fill me still
with nostalgia for
my father's youth.

GERALD GIBSON
Charleston, S. C.

THE TALISMAN

I keep the shell
On the window sill
In the kitchen.
It's only gray
Not pink or pearly
But it fits my hand
Perfectly.
The day I found it
I said
It fits my hand
Perfectly.
Now, whenever I want to,
I hold the shell,
Close my eyes
And feel the Carolina sun.
I look 'way down the beach
And see my children
Tossing bread to the gulls.
I would like to hold the shell
When I die
So I could be assured of
One last side trip
To the sea oats
And the dunes.

ELAINE H. LEONE
Manchester, Connecticut

24

Growing Up So Fast

When I was Eight
I saw a red dead leaf lying on the ground
I picked it up and
rubbed the shriveled death against my innocent cheek
Dusty earth filled my pandorous brain
but I ran and tumbled
through all the leaves across a dewy field
delighted with the change
Leaf after bright leaf after bright dying leaf
I stopped on the edge, gulping excited breaths
The wind slapped my face around
I looked back and
Saw the empty trail made by my feet

LUCY G. LAFFODAY
Clemson, S. C.

On Becoming a Man

Spring and I would go a child,
Sunshine of a wet world, liquid gold;
Vibrant verdant colored carpet;
Fairy-feathered sprites
And magic costumed trees.

My fairy-feathered heart
Lifted legs and arms, an arc,
Salute the sky and dance upon the trees.
Heart give voice and lips obey.
Flaked-fleece firmament record my song
And sing it back to me.

I passed beneath a low-limb oak
Beyond my reach above my head.
An emerald-elf danced on the bough in rhythm to the wind.
My heart leaped up to catch the muse,
But toes, tough tentacles, clung to earth
And bruised my heart against my head.
Frightened fairies, elves, and nymphs forever fled.

PHILIP K. OWEN
Bob Jones University
Greenville, S. C.

SUN TRACKS

My heart wept so I sought the quiet peace of the woods behind my
    house.
The wet leaves were a pungent carpet beneath my feet.
Still my throat ached from withheld tears amid the tumult of
    colorful silence.

Then the sun fired the tops of the poplars high above my head.
Sorrow began to ebb; washed away in a flush of gold.

I walked on; then stopped to pull the weeds from Little Feather's
    grave.
Feather, my gorgeous pet, dead two years now.
The tears came then. Feather gone, a small sorrow but as sharp as
    any . . . . A peg on which to hang a larger sadness.
John is lost too; gone without being absent.

When I looked up I could see the next hill across the way where the
    sun lovingly fingered each gawdy tree before retiring.
Surely to see such a sight is enough.
It is selfish of me to ask for more.

Still the burning need to share a morning's first cup of coffee,
    a sunset or a silent woods with John swamped my reason.
John so tall, so strong and gentle, but never to be mine.
John with love as warm and sparkling, and as fleeting as the sun
    tracks across a blue October sky.

BARBARA N. COLLINS
Pickens High School
Adult Continuation Education
Easley, S. C.

LAST FAREWELL

In the dawn I heard him rise,
Numbed by sleep; and the future bore
Him in her claws, a prize
Exceeding those which came before.

No farewells were to be said,
No good-byes were given us;
We'd said, "Goodnight," and then to bed.
It was his will to leave us thus.

'Twas black as night upon that morn
Of dreary, blackened, rain-smeared sky;
I knew, just as he had been born,
That he would die;

And soon the sun should search
And find him gone
From the chair of his perch,
Lost in war, in early dawn.

A letter came one afternoon;
It simply said,
"Your son was wounded, Wednesday noon."
(No he's dead!)

They brought him home
(On a cold, damp morn)
Enclosed in chrome,
Safe from harm.

I knelt down to touch the chrome,
Then said, "Good-bye . . . and welcome home."

ELIZABETH ANGELL TYSON
Furman University
Greenville, S. C.

Love

"But who would touch first
　　you
　　　　or i"

maybe
>> if we touched
>> black
>> and
>> white
>>> our skins would turn grey
but who would touch first
> you
>> or i

JAMES E. BURNS, JR.
Spartanburg, S. C.

SUPPOSE

Suppose one man were to take one woman to be his bride
To love and to cherish, to share with and be helped by.
Would they remain forever thus?

Suppose love were to draw two unique personalities into a union
Knowing each of their faults, and their needs for a companion.
Would the relationship be static?

If a still-life of Niagara is less desirable than reality
Though both be of water and refract the sun's light,
Why should change be deemed bad?

If the mobility of animals is more noble than a tree's permanance
Though both be called life and creation of more than chance,
Should not dynamics be desired?

Suppose that to know as I am known means that I shall no more find
That sudden revelation when all alone
And searching mysteries complex and divine,

That to experience immutable love requires I stay the very same
And my partner never move
From the hopes and goals as when we first began.

Suppose we couldn't live like that.

Epilogue.
Love is dynamic—it brings changes.
Discovery creates adventure.
Sharing the discovery
          And helping each other discover
               Brings life.

JERRY A. MOBLEY
Clemson, S. C.

(untitled)

His latest lute
Is blonde
He plays her easily
And takes all her light music
Easily, prettily

His fruitiest frump
Is apricot
He devours her nectar
And eats her down to the core
Hungrily, sweetly, completely

His best bitch
Is dark
He finds her in the night
And becomes as black as she
Bumpingly, grindingly, blindingly, mad

His scolding shoe
Is his wife
He tries to put her on
And she creaks and pinches
Lovingly, complainingly
The soul survivor.

MARTHA HEARON
Bishopville, S. C.

(untitled)

Had we but grown up together
Two aching children among the trees
I might not ache like this now,
The long cat-gut note
Strung out tight by the river,
Vibrating, where we should have played.
The reedy banks should have hid us;
We should have cemented our world
With the sticky mud.
We ought to have climbed,
And learned how to reach
And not had this trouble now.

MARTHA HEARON
Bishopville, S. C.

TO YOU

If you feel as I do—you are with me always
in my thoughts and my dreams constantly
until it seems that the beat of my heart is
only for you.

Strange that I should feel the way I do.

And yet, that must be the way of the world
when suddenly and finally you really understand
that life is worth the living for the moment
at hand.

And when the moment is over
the interval between then and death
is only a breath.

JAN WHALEN
Columbia, S. C.

My thoughts bounce with you
and linger mellow on yesterday's bed
of see-saws that balance
old lady beaches and melodrama with
child poems and home-made picture books.

My thoughts move with you
and settle uneasy in dangling certainty
of blackened rocks and child fears
that run to your mind in Sea-Shells
of spider webs.
While you sit in truth-trees and under shaded branches.

JUDY THOMPSON
Columbia, S. C.

36

Growth

Breast to breast, my lips yours enfold;
I gaze through the green waters of your eyes
To the deep corners of your soul,
Lightly obscured by lachrymal ebb and flow that sighs.

Sensitive fingers probe beneath verdant cascades
And tenderly touch damp basecoat of incompleted canvas,
Softly shaping a young spirit of subtle shades
And with gentle stroke altering external cast.

Yet, even as the artist his creation builds,
So becomes he another creature upon leave of easel;
Art and artist, object and maker strike out reborn in
    earthly fields,
Till each, in turn with new master and new subject, shall
    co-mingle.

WILLIAM T. VAUGHAN
University of S. C.
Columbia, S. C.

Ephemera

In late December nights do I
lie scantly on his mind,
as snow too little fallen
to leave footprints in—
as a horn too distant blowing
to be heard against the powdered wind?

On stifled summer nights
when screen doors bang
and insects swarm round
bright bare bulbs,
do his thoughts light
like lightning bugs
on thin grass blades,
turning to me
off and on,
first here, now there,
now gone?

LYNN N. ROBERSON
Converse College
Spartanburg, S. C.

Light trembles along
a golden line
at the edge of night
the haunting spring sings
with a west-wind tongue
waking to a swallow's flight
to the gasp of morning
to the sigh of night
i am the down of fern
the quiver of chilled
grass, nothing more—
in the wings of stars and evening
in the rain-catch of the soul
love, thee, eternity
the only trinity i know.

JILL A. KING
Florence, S. C.

Aspiration

"Finding no fulfillment
But the rewards of eternal quest . . . ."

Four-Fingered Glove

Being idealistic and artistic,
Born into a world of practicality—

Searching for meaning and sense,
Told that virtue is obeying and enduring—

Seeking progress and novel panoramas,
Taught that security harbors in holding to old
   habit and attacking emergent form—

Craving communion of the spirit,
Fed with broth of daily comfort, trunks of worldly
   wealth, and motives of opportunism—

Secretly living a child among men,
   A man among children,
   Finding no fulfillment
   But the rewards of eternal quest . . . .

WILLIAM T. VAUGHAN
University of S. C.
Columbia, S. C.

Reflection

My life has been a fretful trek
Across the endless, treacherous tundra of
Unfulfilled aspirations to rise above
The harsh penury of childhood with
Its unfeeling indifference to my dreams.

With sage advisors guiding my every
Move, I have successfully
Maneuvered through the whitewaters
Of youth, and now I can
Triumphantly display all of the
Accouterments of success.

Yes, I have everything—everything
But contentment—everything but
Fulfillment—everything but peace of mind.
My life has the lustre of an artificial
Gem and the hollow ring of a counterfeit coin.

I'm a wound-up toy man goose-stepping
To the beat of a wound-up toy drum!
Afraid to heed the distant drummer
—What if I should lose all that
For which I have labored—that
Which is valued more by others
Than by me.

Though I'm more afraid, I think,
That I will lose my sense of
Identity—for what am
I stripped of what I possess? Just
Another dreamer who is out of
Step with life.

Ah, but I become so-o weary of
Marching out of step with my
Dreams. I want so desperately to
Achieve great things and dream
Greater dreams.

But wishing will not make
Dreams come true, and I lack
The Courage to count the cadence
That takes me away from the
Life which I have and toward
What I want life to be.

H. BECTON FREE
Columbia, S. C.

Gray mist
still around me
quenches the tiny thirst
of dry brown sway weeds—
as if the sorrow of my soul
might be food
for some seed of time

perhaps a flower of joy.

JOHN HOOE
Wofford College
Spartanburg, S. C.

Sonnet XIII

I hope that I go out as you have done
Spent candle. Bright, you worked at your peak rate
To light my darkened desk, and there are none
To say that you reserved yourself from fate.
Although you knew your span of life was set,
You burned and melted down with equal zeal
In parting moments as when new. You let
Your god, the one who gave you life, conceal
You from oppressing winds that would have blown
You out, and never worried for yourself,
But strove at your appointed task and shone
Throughout the darkest night and poured a wealth
Of light; and serve as well in death, I find,
To be a firm foundation for your kind.

R. GORDON BELL
The Citadel
Charleston, S. C.

47

LOOKING SKYWARD

Delicate smiling winds
Support unwieldy flight
Like pale butterfly wings,
Begun with a countdown
From a child in the meadow.

The wind leaves its taste
Wet and cold in his mouth,
It scampers past him
To eagerly fill the sky
And cajole heavenward his kite.

A swiftly climbing ship
Searching the Olympian plain,
It carries an unspoken prayer
From a young boy who dreams
Of fame and Apollo.

SAMUEL BOYKIN
Seneca, S. C.

LONELY THOUGHTS

The blue mood is upon me again,
And I am dissatisfied with the world.
There is no peace or contentment for
Me now. I long for places I have

Not seen and for friends I have not
Met. To throw off responsibilities
Which I have sought and take
To the open road. Nothing is

Right with me now—I am wrong
With all about me. I will turn from
Everything and everyone and seek myself
On the untraveled ways that beckon.

H. BECTON FREE
Columbia, S. C.

THOUGHTS ON WRITING

For years the urge to write
Has impinged upon my peace of mind
And caused the fingers of my secret self
To frantically clutch the cloak
Of darkness more securely around the
Private me.

For the most part I have been
Successful in keeping it hopelessly buried
Beneath the cluttered demands of the
More immediate tasks at hand, but
In recent months I seem to be losing ground.

The words of my profession
Are more and more elusive, and almost
Daily, now, the urge to write about
feelings and thoughts and people I've met
Wreaks havoc with the challenges at hand.

But I am afraid to write because
To rend the cloak of secrecy which
Protects others as well as me would
Be a step which I could not retrace—
An act I might long regret.

H. BECTON FREE
Columbia, S. C.

SEA GRAVE

Please bury me at sea when I have died,
And feed my body to the hungry deep.
Let my white bones go floating in the tide
When I am come at last to that great sleep.

Return me to the water at my death
To hear the ocean winds that blow above,
For, as my passion was when I had breath,
I'll touch the sandy beaches that I love.

And watch the seabirds slowly dip and soar,
Alone and free, as free as is my soul,
Bowed down and bound by earthly things no more,
A part of all there is, and yet a whole.

So give me then up to the wild, free sea
That I may be of it and it of me.

NELL SHARPE
Columbia, S. C.

A SHRINE

I found a place to worship yesterday,
A tiny room where golden shadows fell
Across the silent space. A mystic spell
Enchanted me and while I paused to pray,
The vibrant tones of music blithe and gay,
Like silver shafts of light that strike the cell
Where lonely, long-forgotten captives dwell,
Released the words of praise my lips would say.

A perfect shrine I found in my retreat,
An altar where the glow of holy fire
Enveloped me and iridescent lay
About the floor to guide my stumbling feet.
It was the crystal peak of my desire,
The place I found to worship yesterday.

EMMA R. BYNUM
Georgetown, S. C.

Observations

"disguised prophets"

Waiting—A Truckstop Poem

Two o'clock
threw itself on the floor
and was ground into the linoleum.
Just another hour like before,
      marble-eyed men slumped
      spellbound through country-twang guitars
      and expresso coffee
      Waiting—
for their beans (jumping Mexicans)
red, blue, yellow.
Highways—
      double yellow streamers
      white band-aid strips
      S's and X's, no U's
      Waiting—
mountains like lumpy pudding
are spread beneath asphalt sheets.
Plowed. Driven between fingers
of hack-drivers.
      Greasy burgers and O-nuts
      roll through. Ammonia paint.
      Disguised prophets:
      scraping grime
      from their fingernails
Waiting—

LANCE J. LEONHIRTH
Wofford College
Spartanburg, S. C.

"Southern Snowfall"

Water-saturated ground crisped and hardened by the cold . . .
Clouds . . . smooth . . . gray, tinged with yellow . . .
"Is that?"
"Yes, it is." . . . An occasional, almost imperceptible
snowflake . . . then nothing.
"Oh, well."
"Look!" Snowfall . . . quiet, a faint rustling on brown leaves.
Increased rapidity, increased size . . . large flakes . . .
floating . . . shattering.
Accumulation . . . whitening pine, forsythia, and doorstep.
Continuing . . . slackening . . . continuing again . . . then—
abruptly—stopping.
The wind rises . . . agitates . . . specter-like images swirling
in wind-blown snow.
Warming trend . . . a quiet, hypnotic dribble trickles from
the roof into an awaiting puddle.
Plunk . . . plunk . . . plash.
Momentary beauty . . . evanescent . . . ephemeral . . .
completely vanished.

JARED C. (Jay) EVATT
Clemson University
Central, S. C.

First Frost

The cold dryness from the half-opened window
Twitched in my nostrils and woke me
And as I first opened my eyes
Thought, yes, maybe today
And shivered with cold and expectation
Standing barefoot on the hard pine floor
Before putting on shoes and going out for the paper

It is; it has come
The grass crunching underfoot
Like the sound of hard breakfast cereal
Munched inside your head
The loose red dirt, along the wall
Where no grass grows
Frozen in intricate designs
As if some Renaissance ants had been busy
A young Michelangelo sculpturing or
Perhaps da Vinci fortifying
But the breast-works are so brittle
And the miniature towers crumble at a touch

J. R. LONG
University of S. C., Spartanburg
Greenville, S. C.

Snow

Snow falls but little
Here in the South
And when it does
Those who live on hills
Thinking of their comings and goings
Mutter "Godammit to hell"
Under their breath
As they go up to the attic
To bring down
Sleds for the children

J. R. LONG
University of S. C., Spartanburg
Greenville. S. C.

Like so many dead leaves
Obligated to the whim of a sudden wind,
They scraped along the ground
Or perhaps for one swift moment
Shot high into the air,
Until,
Crunching some beneath his feet,
Someone raked them into a pile,
Scooped them up,
And
Carried
Them
Away.

RHETT S. THURMAN
Charleston, S. C.

SHELLS

Some were like old bones,
Bleached and broken
And very wise.
Some were hewn, some bright,
And some were smooth and cool.
One was perfect. A symphony.
With its own, intimate being
Each one had cried out
(If only to me)
From the multitudes and damp weed,
"Touch me."
"Turn me over."
"Hold me to your cheek."
And all of them,
Each and every one of them,
Smelled of life.

RHETT S. THURMAN
Charleston, S. C.

SHOOTING RATS

Scrambling on the burned lip of a trash barrel,
nose twitching, shaking with food smell;
eyes, nervous eyes, in all directions.
Now body fat with garbage
hanging on front sight blade.
Breathe, set, aim, squeeze . . .
High in the air squealing;
after the shot it
happens slowly,
slowly turning,
slowly, the apex,
frozen—red ember eyes
snapped out,
stub feet splayed to the four corners
as if, drying, the skin were tacked to a wall;
piece of torn dripping grease flesh.
I am not the same man for joy.

LUCAS CARPENTER
Charleston, S. C.

Pipe Dream

Torn bits of melody in the light black cafe
A Five-o-clock shadow lights dense brown tobacco.
   It swirls blindly until
      it hits a shaft of spotlight
      and a sweeping slow-motion breeze
It bends in transparent cat-calm curls
        Sensuously stretching into thin air

LUCY G. LAFFODAY
Clemson, S. C.

62

6 o'clock

acidic newsreels
gnaw
the tough of my sole
            tho' tramp the festering pictures
            of lust and loss
            I do
holes betray my calloused guards
and send me screaming
            crudely oozing corrupt innuendos—
relief for decay?   no
the fisted blacks and shifty browns and gooky reds
are not renowned for talk!

and so I sit before my set
a teeming lump of disgust

a victim of circumstance

JOHN HOOE
Wofford College
Spartanburg, S. C.

In Salem's Cemetery

In an hour left unplanned,
While the moon shone bright and grand,
Went my friend and I to creep
Among the graves of those who sleep.
There we told some tales new
Of ghostly things some say are true.
And as we paced on paths of stone,
Observing how the trees were blown,
And thinking of the time when we
Would be laid there, our souls set free,
We came on markers of all sorts,
Bearing us the good reports
Of those who had been buried there,
The elder ones and maidens fair.
It happened that my friend called me
To kneel with him upon one knee,
To look at what he had just found,
A certain little grassy mound.
The stone was simple, plain and white,
Reflecting well the full moon's light.
Of the name I took no note,
Nor of the four short lines they wrote.
But the birth of him who lay
Had been ten years ago that day.
And on that soft green grassy mat
A cake with ten small candles sat.
Of its bearer we found no clue,
Just mother's tears among the dew.

R. GORDON BELL
The Citadel
Charleston, S. C.

The Late Show

Floating transluscent images
etch prophesies and memories
on blackened, corroded pages.
Silence hammers hollow echoes
as forgotten faces project
kaleidoscopically.
Translation of message not understood.
Tarnished metal and rotten wood.

JIM R. BAZEMORE
Rock Hill, S. C.

Wonder

"what awaits . . . at the river's unknown end"

"WATER UNTO WATER"

Flowing, tossed down this prodigious river
Each a tributary to this faceless stream.
Fast currents bounding over endless falls
Knowing slowness only in the few lulls
        of peaceful shores
Lacking knowledge of nearing mystery-laden bends
Nor grasping the dangers of quick sharp rapids
We journey silently onward with hopeful dreams
Of what awaits the faithful at the rivers
        unknown end.
Would so longingly we aspire if we knew
        the ocean's yearn
Was to whisper life's simple axiom:
        water unto water?

GERALD W. SMITH
Columbia, S. C.

THE SHEDDING OF SKIN

I

In sleep beyond nativity, he curls
Himself and slightly nods because immersed:
The wet star in his liquid universe—
Suspended, drowned aloof from colder worlds
Beyond his temperate amniotic dream.
The tiny god who reigns within the cell
Has come to bear this embryonic swell
As witness to some vast vertebral theme.
A thousand skins lie strewn along the path,
The relics of his time-mutated growth:
The gills and fangs and tails became minute
With each successive moult. The aftermath
Reveals him pared by his genetic oath
For birth: a freshly-peeled and glistening fruit.

II

Secure beyond eternity, the fresh
Deceased is glowing bright as if yet warm.
Once borne erect like suffering, his flesh
Is dry and numb and shielded from all harm.
But shovelled in his melting place, he strains
To join his thwarted bloodless knees and head—
The tight instinctive curve, secure from pain.
The sagging flesh begins to peel and shred . . .
A fluid heat engulfs the fecund tomb
And all within begins to swell and groan.
The dead one drowns and curls within the womb,
Astonished by the brilliance of his bones.

His final skin shrugged free beneath the earth,
He shivers in his coil and burns for birth.

DONALD R. BELT, JR.
A. C. Flora High School
Columbia, S. C.

AQUARIUS

There aren't as many ways to see
how things happen as one might think,
and loathsome logic will be
none the worse for it.
Once the chickens have flown the coop,
and the farmer is left with stupid mouth
as his corn or wheat or whatever dives
back into the dirt and covers up, there
can be no more benedictions for the crying.
And one look at the twofold age of man
will silence finally a mouldering faith,
for History comes, offering an open hand,
while Entropy leads his own untuned band.

LUCAS CARPENTER
Charleston, S. C.

I leaned on
Your porch steps,
One hand hidden
In a torn pocket,
And watched
The gray-blue smoke
Of my cigarette
Furl softly up
And vanish.
With each thin whirl
An ennui rose
Around me
Shredding
The empty husk
Of night
Into quiet, black
Ashes.
Then, in the house,
A thing trembled;
It was nothing—
Absence
Finality
Your death—
Nothing,
A pale hollow now,
A gentle trembling
Of your absence;
And time seemed
To snow down,
   Slowly,
  Through the
  Thick
  Silence
  Of my
  Loneliness.

ERIC G. HARTLEY
Columbia, S. C.

AFTERNOON WITH RAIN

All this grey, dripping credence,
a river in the crown,
stepping its way, in spasms,
up the brown hill to a white house
certain after a hundred years of solitude.
The house waits. A blue bowl waits, incomplete.
The absurdity of a bowl or crown turned
upside down in the afternoon.
It rains only in the afternoon,
and the river in the crown
is swelled from blue acceptance.
The wind behind the rain blows through it,
beginning and end of the white house
with people waiting as the rain breaks through
the thunderstorm of sun. The house,
certain after a hundred years of solitude;
the people, frozen by the blizzard of the sun,
thawed slowly by the rain.

LUCAS CARPENTER
Charleston, S. C.

IMPRISONED

You can't see it, but you know it's there;
It's been put up one brick at a time—
Brick, Mortar, Brick, Mortar, Brick—
Layer after layer, until it's soared above hand and head,
Out of reach, but never out of sight.
It's as real to you as the clanging of
    metal against metal, steel against steel,
    key against lock.

Life has no key; death has no pardon.
There's not even a changing of the guard;
There's no one to take the place;
    no time to replace one evil for another.
Others within the wall are blind. You see,
    but what is the good of it?
Can one eye open all minds, one mind tear down
    brick and mortar that it has put up itself?

What escape is there for one who builds his own wall?
The wall won't fall of itself.
The winds and storms of life strengthen it
Until it roots and grows.
Must you learn to be content—sit in the corner
    until you too root and grow?
Take your seat nearby.
The soil is rich and the rain is free.

DAVE WILSON
Tigerville, S. C.

SUNGLASSES ON A CLOUDY DAY

Monday mornings are cloudy days
   filled with Sunday's children
wearing Sunglasses.   Polaroid
       people shed the glares
  of Darkness.
Shades shield Sunrays
   from insensitive eyes;
  Empty   eyes   evade
    the arrival of empty light
As the least of the little children

                  look

     longing to see the Sun,
but are forced to file with
Family and friends wearing
    Sunglasses on cloudy days.

The human effort—how strange!
Your strength is spent
   in useless efforts of hypocrisy.
Tell me who you are
        that I might hopefully
    see the truth.
Your young yearn in desperation
      for the same truth as I—
        shaded by nothing;
But the truth is tinted
      and your youth cry
      for those who wear
No Sunglasses on cloudy days.

DAVE WILSON
Tigerville, S. C.

Beach—In Winter

A ragged windswept wedge of geese fly south
Through sullen mist, which magnifies the cold.
The summer crowds, sun worshippers, are gone.
The lonely, ever-moving sea seems old.

Our footprints in the sand will vanish with the flooding
tide.
And memory alone can hold this moment free.
As all the summer footprints now are gone,
Cloaked by the sombre, ever-changing sea.

Will you and I, like footprints in the sand
Exist a brief and passing moment and be gone?
No. Like the sea, we change our mood and temper now and then
But we exist for all the years to come.

MORRIS C. LUMPKIN
Columbia, S. C.

IDYLL FOR DOE HALL

Grey sand
stretching, stretching,
reaching out toward a sea.
Leaping, leaping
over marsh pools,
islands of grass.
I see this
I hear beyond, sea sounds.
I think this, infinitely.
Standing, standing
ALONE
in this intoxication
of your marsh margin,
a place unpeopled.
"Heron-priested" on edges or knee-deep,
fishing, fishing.
Swallowing, swallowing comically
not startled by
ME,
unmoving, unmoving,
softly calling, calling your name.
Disturb this idoneous landscape?
No, no.
Follow a path, quietly.
Leave under heaven
what is
heaven's doing.

Legend: upon finding no one at home.
Read slowly, slowly—here is magic.

KAY C. SISSON
Columbia, S. C.

I MUST HAVE A PLACE

I could not see him reduced to ash. Let
It happen underground, if it must,
An ecclesiastical return to dust.
I must have a place upon this earth square
Enough to stand upon
And say he is from here to here. Yet
I hate this narrow
Architecture
Down to the marrow
Gray stones,
Down to the milk
White bones,
Down to the silk—
Lined box that made my mother poor.
He should lie
At home in the side yard where
He used to sit in beneficent sun.
There is little comfort in the stare
Of crumbling angels row on row
And granite cannot hold his history;
Still I choose this over nothing. I
Must have a place of absolute geography
Where my father is, where of necessity
I go.

GRACE POW SIMPSON
Georgetown, S. C.

THIS VITAL SEA

All the cliches are here—those inevitable changing tides,
Shifting sands, even the calm before the storm;
And for those of livelier bent, wild oats
(All right to sow, but prohibited by law to reap).
Why then do I come back another season,
When most exasperated with accustomed turns,
Of attitude as well as phrase? Perhaps because
It's easy to conjecture Columbus out of history
And nullify the platitudes a round new world recites
In such simplicity of water, sand and sky.
I can will the artificial backdrop there
(Too bright a blue to be believed)
To get obediently wet in that
Far meeting place upon the rim;
Can watch the sailboats slip across the edge
And hear the gulls skriek naked epitaphs.

I'll not deprecate this sea's capacity
With shallow contemplation of its depth.
There are no intellectual questions here—
Those early stirring creatures moved by instinct to the land
As I am moved by instinct back again.
If I could specify the agent of my death
I'd take the sea. *Water thou art* if better
Science than dry dust and biblical as Jordan.
Meanwhile I'd like to feel my passions rage
And reach flood tide again for any cause,
To be blood-brother to this vital sea
And taste the same salt breaking through my veins.

GRACE POW SIMPSON
Georgetown, S. C.

Ariadne Abandoned

The dolphin herds of Amphitrite's train
Leap sprightly through the blue Aegean Sea.
And over sleeping infant waves, the free
And soaring birds glide to Arion's strains;
They softly float in air and seem as reins,
Guiding the ocean host melodiously,
While Neptune's horses prance, anemone
Adorned, with brazen hoofs and golden manes.
But silently, upon the foam-kissed strand,
Abandoned Ariadne stands forlorn
And watches drowsily the pageant pass
And wonders why she slept upon the sand
And why her lover left her there that morn
And what the black sail means that Theseus has.

TERRY L. NORTON
Clemson University
York, S. C.

```
        S
S       N           E
  N       O       K
    O       O   A
      W W L
SNOWFLAKE
        W L L
      O   A   A
    N   K     K
  S     K       E
        E
```

From dusty vapor
To six-sided perfection,
Waiting patiently for a cue.
The stage is set.
Cast of thousands enter
In silent choreography,
Piling into an exhausted mass.

A one-run bomb.

DECK GUESS
Union High School
Union, South Carolina 29379

Portraits

"they were still strangers"

A PICTURE OF PARENTS WITHOUT CHILDREN

She would sew
        new thoughts,

           beads,
into the many-colored pattern of memory

and he would solder
          older thoughts of his own into place . . .

    Long ago
they had learned to slaughter
              laughter
and to tear
      tears from each's other.

But. There had been a time   , once,
when they were still strangers to anger;
    There had been a time
when they could lie sun-baked
            naked upon the sand
or lie lower than the flowers
or bow low upon their own brown bearskin
    beside the hearth
          unearthing new treasures
    from their together,
and for many an hour
          pour their love
from lip to mouth
like milk from a pitcher
to a glass.

But that time passed.

DUANE VORHEES
Charleston Heights, S. C.

THE CIRCLE

A real Whither-Thou-Goest girl and an Ideal Mother,
She was a huge polar bear
Lumbering the limits of
Her own private glacier
Of husband-and-child.

How conveniently she decided that her Purpose In Life
Was to please men, and thus enforced
She went to Serve, armed with
Eyelash, Dimple, and Psoriasis.

Another, enjoying what she called Harmless Flirtation,
Mulled over that Purpose, thought it sounded
Pretty Good, and took it as Her Own.

She even *listened* timidly, making no motion except perhaps
To adjust dark glasses against The Glare, or
Re-cross her ever-socked feet.
She listened as we swapped Continent Stories,
Having none of her own.
European Driving gave her Diarrhea.

In jersey white and gold earring,
She bore a resemblance to Mr. Clean.

With Smug Sophistication she related her Countless Conquests,
Relying confidently on her Freckles
To counterbalance her Insufferable Wisdom.

Jack of All Trades, Master of None, she collected characteristics
For Observation, but let them go Unharmed,
Clinging only to what she called My Identity,
And grimly hoping that when she said, "It is I,"
It would be.

RHETT S. THURMAN
Charleston, S. C.

His Trowel

He left his hoe and trowel
by the toolshed door.
He needs them no more.

From the wheelbarrow's edge
runs a ribbon of slime;
the dawn makes known the snail's
night-climb to heights the day denies him.
The Japanese beetles are busy,
huddled inside a white chrysanthemum,
satyr-like,
their puddle of black appetite
busy.
The lady bug lights and looks and leaves
the grey weathered gate which grieves
as a rabbit hops through
for fresh lettuce leaves—
a fine breakfast.
The beaded red raspberries
plump with dew
are ripe today that were yesterday new,
and the ground is quick
with living things,
and the air with brief bursts of wings.

But his hoe and trowel
are still
by the toolshed door.
His garden may grow as it will,
he guards it no more.

LYNN N. ROBERSON
Converse College
Spartanburg, S. C.

THE FORK-LIFT

The day that Bodie Harris lost his leg
Began like any other working day.
At six he left his weather-blistered shack
And steered the thirty-seven crooked miles
Of U. S. 1 from Blaney to his job.
At seven sharp he punched the sacred clock
The way he'd done for twenty-six long years,
Ambled up, across the barren lumber yard,
And climbed upon his cold metallic throne.
They'd worked together quite a while, those two,
Moving two-ton wooden blocks of banded planks
Like firewood from the boxcars to the bins.
His cracked brown hands were swollen by the years
Of throbbing cold, yet strange and gentle with the gears
And wheel of that collosal strength machine.
Majestic through the sheds he'd proudly whirl
His beast and shine that silly grizzled grin.

It seemed more than betrayal of a friend
When Bodie slipped between the heavy blades
And they slammed down and pinned him in the dust.
As if the lift, a patient yellow fiend,
Had waited years for such a perfect chance
To crush the tiny thing that rode its back
All day and twisted it to wake and sleep,
Prodded it to strain and lift each timber mass,
And fed its hungry gut with butane gas.

DONALD R. BELT, JR.
University of S. C.
Columbia, S. C.

Humor

"I am a Gypsy, sir,
And cannot play the violin!"

While on my way to Oberlin
I met a man bowed down with care.
Great tears fell dripping from his chin
And splashed about him everywhere.

Said I, "You scarce seem tipsy, sir,
Whatever caused the grief you're in?"
Sobbed he, "I am a Gypsy, sir,
And cannot play the violin!"

MABEL H. FISCHER
Beaufort, S. C.

GREAT THINKERS, UNITE!

my mind just dropped a bomb.
it hit the ground
with a terrific explosion
and made my shoes all messy.

an ant crawled through the rubble
and came out reciting
the Pythagorean Theorem.
a thirsty dog came up and drank—
coating his throat with the wreckage,
and he left while giving me
his opinions of the world situation.

after several intelligent conversations
with a grasshopper,
a snake,
and a Japanese beetle,
i began to marvel
at the great change
i had launched for the world.

my thoughts were interrupted
by a man who came up
and told me
to clean up the mess i had made.

DEBORAH SUE KEISTER
Beaufort High School
Burton, S. C.

"Riddle"

I wonder how fat people
Really rotund
Ever manage to make love

Or is rubbing stomachs just as satisfying?

OKSANNA NAHNYBIDA
Charleston, S. C.

"GIRLS AND BOYS"

LITTLE GIRLS WITH BIG BLUE EYES
LITTLE BOYS OF THE RIGHT-TYPE SIZE
ARE TOO SOON
BIG GIRLS WITH LONG TAN THIGHS
BIG BOYS WITH THE RIGHT TYPE LIES

GERALD W. SMITH
Columbia, S. C.

A NOTED POET
ADVERSELY VERSED
ABOUT A BOUT
OF WINTER FLU

SURVIVED HIS POEM
BUT HE SUCCUMBED
TOO SOON TO EARN
HIS DULY DUE

"POSTHUMOROUS POEM"

GERALD W. SMITH
Columbia, S. C.

UMPHLETTISMS*

Straight
And what is that to crooked
And why produced it so.
Huh.
Relative to what we find said regularity
And its relative commulative historicity.
Suppose that the thing did exist
In a setting of sameness with it all around.
Possibly—to help, of course
Of course   —the
Straight were crooked
Perverted   , different
Extremely   . Then
Would straight be straight or French curve?
Should same be like or different?
Would I be me, you, he, or she?   So what?
While you chew the fat and methodically
Speak on where it's at
(Or where it was when last you chewed—
Or was it spat?)
And counter point with opposing point
And guise it all in honesty,
I give, search, hope, try;
I'm asked a million reasons why.

The wheels here are aturnin'—
The functions afunction' Fine;
Too bad that we folks lack the use
Of what all's inside that mind!

JERRY A. MOBLEY
Clemson, S. C.

*The title is taken from a person's name, Margaret Umphlett, who has, in my opinion, the uncanny ability to make something out of nothing.

MY HEART LEAPS UP WHEN I BEHOLD
(Let The Ladies Have Their Sway)

"A Texas doctor says that women who wiggle when they walk are affecting the motion. An actress fires back that they are not affecting at all—that the effect is natural."

Every lad who loves a lass sets
Prideful store upon her assets
And he likes to think her swing's *au natural.*

But if it is affected,
Just a motion she's perfected—
Does it really make a difference, after all?

For an artful undulation,
Syncopated with gyrations,
Is a movement with a meaning all its own.

And there are no buts about it,
Not a lass should be without it—
Lack of exercise might leave a stern untoned.

CHARLES G. JOYNER
Myrtle Beach, S. C.

LOS ANGELES-(AP)-Henceforth, anyone in the United States planning "activities aimed at modifying the weather" must, by law, give 30 days advance notice to the National Science Foundation or face a fine of up to $500 . . .

The new regulation applies to such modern wizardry as "seeding" clouds—efforts to produce rain, prevent hail or break up hurricanes.

In the late 1940's responsible scientists demonstrated they could occasionally produce rain by seeding certain clouds with tiny particles of dry ice, silver iodide or liquid propane . . .

My garden needed water
So I planned to make it rain
By seeding clouds with iodide, dry ice, liquid propane.
But the National Foundation now has made it very plain
That if I do, the heavy dew had better fall in Spain.

Else I'll face a fine for failing to give notice in advance—
One MUST give unfair warnings when rain is not left to chance,
For to plan precipitation, unpermitted, is unlawful.
(Presumably, with a permit, one may make the weather awful.)

NOTE: I plan to make it rain upon the 31st of May
(Unless that is a day on which the Dodgers are to play).
But if they play, and it's not fair, I will not be to blame.
—My rain will be called on account of the game.

CHARLES G. JOYNER
Myrtle Beach, S. C.

Youth

"for I will carry you across fields of
wonder, and broken waters"

FOR I LOVE THEE

I will wander through the woods
And, if I get lost
Your hand will reach out and touch mine
       to show me the way.
You will show me the way, won't you?
Yes, for I've trust in the love you
       have instilled in me.
We've come to a clearing now,
And your hand does reach out to help
       me across the broken waters,
The broken waters of my mind.
And you say, "Be still my poppet,
for I will carry you across fields of
       wonder, and broken waters,
For, I love thee."

LORI ANNE PIERCE
Irmo Middle School
Columbia, S. C.

BEGINNING: 6:33

The sun spills
      with a freshness
            upon the floor
      melting the darkness
            to unfold the dawn.

Newborn fingers of the day ahead
    reach out
            to capture
            the fleeing moments

holding them but a second
            then setting them free
      yielding to watch
                each moment
                    drift
                into the prisms
                    of life.

MELANIE LEIGH BOLEMAN
Columbia High School
Columbia, S. C.

The rosemary

We must have met before—and loved—
    perhaps eras ago in some timeless place.
For how else could your face,
your eyes, hands and voice
be so familiar to me?

    Perhaps some other time you have held me
    and we have found comfort in each other.
How else could such a bond
(as that between us) have been formed?

Love was always—it is not new to us.
And I cannot believe that we
    were thrown together by chance.
No, we must have met before—and loved—
    for you are not strange to me.

PATRICIA WILSON
St. Andrew's Parish High School
Charleston, S. C.

fall

if colored leaves are to your liking
i'll bundle up the piles
and gently sprinkle them
upon your mountain path

if i am to your liking
then you do the bundling
and sprinkle me wherever you are

MYRNA GORDON
Lugoff-Elgin High School
Lugoff, S. C.

between snowflakes

i don't profess to be an
expert on the concept of loving or a
prophet
i really don't know what makes a heart beat faster or
breathing come harder
i only know that my heart now is yours and that this
feeling of never wanting to entrust it to
another does not escape me
i've heard the whining of snow falling
sideways in the corners of my silence and i've
stretched my fingers wide and watched
how their warm touch could destroy this
white silent unrepeatable thing and
i've cried for what has
been and for what has been no more
i've praised the intervals of having been touched . . . of
having had someone revealed to me and
now while balling my fists and staring out from
whatever i've become with time i am
resolving between snowfall and
snowflake to separate the warm from the cold . . .

if it melts . . . let it be by its own undoing . . .
if you go . . . leave silently as the snow . . .

MYRNA GORDON
Lugoff-Elgin High School
Lugoff, S. C.

icicle trees

    icicle trees
have frozen joints and creaky bones.
      they break and swish a crunchy leaf
      and let it fall and chip the ground.
dance, dance   in short sharp steps
      and strip yourself in the wind,
      and cry with melty tears, dripping icicle trees,
make my eyelashes freeze when you cry on me.

ELLEN DEAS BOYKIN
Joseph Kershaw Academy
Rembert, S. C.

Christmas Poem

If I could be Santa Claus, what would I do?
Why, I would go from one house to another—
filling stockings, giving presents to you.

If I could be Santa what would I do?
I would give a present to you.
Candy canes, and planes, and trains.
That's all I would give to you.

BRAD KEVIN BOXEY (Age 8)
Irmo Middle School
Columbia, S. C.

YESTERDAY

Yesterday the rain called to me,
And said come with me,
And I went.

We went to the marsh,
And played and danced,
And sang, and sang, and sang.

We went to the river,
And the sea beyond,
And pegged the surface,
As the waves rolled.

We laughed and cried,
And whispered, and shouted,
And suddenly stilled,
I returned all alone.

WILLIAM W. POWELL
Porter-Gaud School
Charleston, S. C.

Bumblebees

Bumblebees.
They just know how to make it sound
As if the world is peeking into windows all around
And the winds blow holes in clouds.

Catching the eyes of all in all,
And dancing with ladies who have no feet,
And washing in soapless water,
And making bubbles out of air
To them is so easy.

It's unfair
To have them stare at me
And know that I can't even walk just right
While they smoothly captivate all who hear or see.
And fly with frosted wings
Away from all the quests of ours.

They find and construe the faith in God:
Dance and hope with humming, breathless victor's song
To have only purple and fine linen.
And softly settle into sweet and smiling pink.
And become a victim of it all.
And die,
Of a broken heart.

ELLEN DEAS BOYKIN
Joseph Kershaw Academy
Rembert, S. C.

Lingering,
foot poised
above the stair,
reluctantly
descending
from upstairs worlds
to
greasy dishes,
stale newspapers
and cigarette butts,
runny noses
and monday squabbles,
burnt toast
and missing socks.
Hesitating,
feet pausing,
she sighs
and
continues
down
to greet
the
morning.

BONNIE CAMPBELL
Christ Church High School
Greenville, S. C.

110

my child,

    if I could only take your burdens
      upon my willing shoulders!
        but I cannot,
  for your burdens will make you strong.

    if I could only show you all I've seen
      and felt and learned!
        but I cannot,
  for you must find life for yourself.

    if I could only give you treasures and gifts
      to fill your life with beauty!
        but I cannot,
  for you must learn that life is hard.

    I can never understand you,
    for your world is not my world.
    I can never expect any return,
    for that would bind your freedom,

but I can give you beauty & pain & knowledge
  & love & strength & laughter & tears
    because, my child,
  I gave you life.

BONNIE CAMPBELL
Christ Church High School
Greenville, S. C.

floating from town to town,
    from friend to friend,
I have grown adept at
    opening and closing,
    laughing and crying,
    gaining and losing.

I have lived the extremes
and missed the mundane

but somehow, this time,
    I have gained too much
    and opened too far
(perhaps I stayed too long)

for this time the loss will be
    bigger than I
    and when I leave,
        I will not open again

        easily
        or painlessly.

BONNIE CAMPBELL
Christ Church High
Greenville, S. C.

Measure Me, Sky

Measure me, sky,
Am I so infinitely small,
so immeasurable
Am I nothing?
I look at you and all your starry wonder,
and I see that I am nothing, yes, nothing . . .

Measure me, sky,
Measure my mind.
Am I so wise, so smart?
I say I am so wise, but is it true?
I claim to be king of all on Earth, but is it true?
I claim to be so organized with all of my government and
rules, but am I?
No, for even the bees are as organized as I.
And does a king kill his servants with all of his
waste and pollution?

Measure me, sky,
Measure my soul.
Am I so spiritually better than the least of your kingdom?
Isn't it true that even the chicken thanks you for every drink of
water it takes.
Yes, 'tis true . . . I am only a creature no better than the least.

JERRY CHARLES BISHOP
Middleton High School
Charleston, S. C.

YELLOW WEDNESDAY'S HEROES

Each man to his novel ways
   and so the earth will turn again
   and never will we feel a repetitious day.

A body has his chosen fears
   and carries his image-loves
And no one has yet been born who will dictate to another
         the one who will be his true hero.

Each man has his heroes,
   in all the broken bits of world, distinction prevails.
   a one in single mind of minutes
   plays the song inside the brain
   and once again the tune is welded—the birth of a hero.

To every lonely soldier, each month holds directed space
   on the huge and spinning wheel of only a year.
No one north and no one south is always true.
   the seer of the hours is the only soul
   to know the placement of the month in his own eyes.

One seventh of a week holds a color of its own.
Monday in its pallid white lies dying in his open tomb
And Tuesday blue will always be the strange one.
Friday's air must redden in my eyes,
   because she always stands with her own favorite red deception
   while Yellow Wednesday's heroes
         crawl upon the wall.

ELLEN DEAS BOYKIN
Joseph Kershaw Academy
Rembert, S. C.

Swan Sonnet

When song invites to flee to higher glades,
Pretended horses with my broom are stilled.
For ink I find me lay aside my spades
To polish necks of swans which I have quilled.
Gray swan to swan, the mood is sketched in grace.
It lulls my mind to wander where it will
And feather, beak, and wing become your face,
And passion seeks the freedom of the quill.
Though higher glades clinch all the days in snow,
The thought of swan to be flesh of your soul
Will wrap you warm with soft and subtle glow
And sweeten life to you and keep it whole.
And never will my love cage coming dawns
But only make them free with flight of swans.

ELLEN DEAS BOYKIN
Joseph Kershaw Academy
Rembert, S. C.

apple core

worthless little bits of darling baby lines.
they fall down through my hollow arms
    and through my hands, out of my pencil
        on to steady sheets.
stable tables count us each day before we go to bed,
    and say that we may live with another million
    with only square inches for each toe.
with closing ears and listening eyes,
I top the skies.
    waxen angels care for me there,
    and on to weaker times.
I rest my head against the tree
    with the heavy thoughts of nothing
    bearing down upon my head to kill me there.
I know that one day I will die in bed,
    an apple core with no surrounding skin,
    and all of my good eaten away.

ELLEN DEAS BOYKIN
Joseph Kershaw Academy
Rembert, S. C.

Alone

I stand alone, bracing myself against the biting
cold that forces me to pull my faded jacket
tight around my stiff body;
As the icy wind stings my face and numbs my
fingers, I hear soft voices floating through
the park,
I wait . . .
The wind moans and then hushes,
all is quiet.
I kick a can and bite my lips at the pain
that shoots up my toes.
As the clanging sound echoes away, I hear
footsteps briskly approaching;
Distant voices become clear and audible,
I see smiling faces and hear full laughter
I too smile and begin to laugh.
The smiling faces melt into frozen hate as
they stare at me,
As I turn to leave I hear the word, "black"
followed by cruel laughter.
The sounds die away
And I stand alone.

MARTHA MONTGOMERY RHODES
Lake City High School
Lake City, S. C.

117

Childhood—

                                        gone forever.
But the memories remain.
It's even permissible to take them out
        and relive them
        from time to time.
I know a little shop
    where you can rent pogo sticks by the hour
    and chew pink bubble gum
    and giggle
    and make sand castles.
The clerk will sell you purple pinewheels
        but he'll tell you
        his specialty is cranberry kites.
They're cheap on Wednesdays during Spring,
    and everyone past childhood buys one.
There's magic in those cranberry sails—
Somehow,
        when you're running through a meadow,
        bright-eyed and short of breath,
Head thrown back to watch tossing sails of crimson,
Childhood—

                                seems possible.

                    ROBIN BARNETT
                    Union High School
                    Union, S. C.

118

Daydreams

Slow, sliding, slippery *earth*,
turning, burning *silently*,
escaped my grasp as it *slipped*
and broke the barriers *past*
enduring moments of *time*.

Lonely, lovely sight *leaving*
memories that seemed to *me*,
mixed with thoughts forever *lost*
to a mind encompassed *in*
my dreary, dwindling *dreams*.

JULIA WHITE
St. Andrew's High
Charleston, S. C.

Meditation on Myself

When I get older
And sit
With folded hands
I'll want to remember myself
   like the rain.
Sometimes unpredictable
   or mischievous.
Sometimes simple—
   but free.
Trying perhaps,
   to fill a puddle
With little drops of life
And asking why—
   in its reflection—
My dreams
   must float away.

SUSIE STRICKLAND
Joseph Kershaw Academy
Camden, S. C.

I often dream of being an aging sailor
in the middle of the silent
    sea
With land not
    visible;
 With no one to watch me
    but the
      sun;
 With no one to push me
    but the
      wind.

BRAD BYCE
Westside High School
Anderson, S. C.

Epitaph

Yea,

and unto this universe
was brought forth
this virgin earth

and mankind
did rape the earth
to prove his virility.

Reveling in self-satisfaction,
with no thought of love or return,
he took her all . . .

and finally he stood back,
angered that she could give
no more.

Then, aghast, he recognized
the fragile spirit he had shattered
and saw what he had wrought,

and yea,

he wept.

BONNIE CAMPBELL
Christ Church High
Greenville, S. C.

122

I can see
a campfire
covering the countryside,
large enough
for everyone in the world
to make a circle around it.
I can hear us all singing
folk songs
of our own composition,
and I can hear
grasshoppers
applauding in the distance.
we are passing
marshmallows and cocoa
among us,
some are playing guitars and harmonicas,
others are tapping their feet.
a very good night
for the end of the world.

TIM HEDGECOTH
Hillcrest High School
Sumter, S. C.

Recycling Day

The americanly ubiquitous station-wagon
passengered with its quota of four kids
stuffing their mouths
with Cocoa Krispies and Lucky Charms
drives up to unload boxes
filled with four weeks of
newspapers, glass jars, tin cans,
    and the cardboard tubes from toilet tissue.

As the car, disburdened, drives out
into the street,
one kid throws his empty cereal box
out the back window.

GENIE FLOYD
Hartsville Senior High
Hartsville, S. C.

Simon

      Simon,
it's been a long time since I've been remembering you.
    You are a summer's child,
with black night hair
      in baby soft curls
      floating around your shoulders.
And you laugh away the days of lonely lovers
      with a smile of faded blush lips,
      lips to kiss a forehead.
Bronze cheeks are your face,
they hold your homesick eyes—
      large drops of glossy melted chocolate.

You never walk.
You flow,
      with the polish of an artist.
Your olive dark-lined body
           is tall,
           as slender as a strong, young pine,
           and leaves your subtle shadows.

      Simon,
you tower over everyone,
      but with the slightest warmth,
      you melt into a soft, young boy
      and your homesick eyes become sweet, rippled pools.

ELLEN DEAS BOYKIN
Joseph Kershaw Academy
Rembert, S. C.

Indian Charlie and His Arrow

Do you remember when you shot me?
I remember.
I ran between almost every tree and fence to get away,
            but you caught me still.
      that was funny,
I loved you, but you shot me
   and I know that you must remember.

Charlie, find your bow
   and let's go out again today like we did then.
I think you hurt my head, though.
You shot me in the forehead with your arrow.
   a piece of it is still there and I think it.
   I put it in my back pocket and I speak it.

I bled on my white shirt
   and you were the only one who cared
   and who wrapped your red neck tie around my eyes
         so I wouldn't see me bleed.
I'm sorry that you lost your arrow, Charlie,
   I wanted you to teach me to be an Indian.

ELLEN DEAS BOYKIN
Joseph Kershaw Academy
Rembert, S. C.

A TRIBUTE TO ALBERT EINSTEIN

i am a mushroom.
my mind stretches across the horizon—
spreading my ideas
and housing intricate memories;
my stem reaches far down into the ground—
reaching and violently grasping
every conceivable element,
in order to stay alive.
i am the fungus of struggle,
and i adhere to man's weakness.

DEBORAH SUE KEISTER
Beaufort High School
Burton, S. C.

POSEIDON

Upon the humped back of a whale he rides—
Poseidon with his sixteen pronged spear—
Ready to strike against the cold black night—
Lying, waiting in the depths so still—
The iced black whale of evil carries him
Into the darkness, quietly it swims
And leaving not a hint nor a trace to be found—
Down he goes, using the bold ocean holds—
He waits for the unconceived event
For his intent is only to prevent—

Poseidon, not born or formed from any god
But by the demon creature, mortal man—

KEMP DUDLEY BOX
Porter-Gaud School
Charleston, S. C.